The Shadow of Sirius

Also by W.S. Merwin

W.S. MERWIN

The Shadow of Sirius

Copper Canyon Press

Port Townsend, Washington

Grateful acknowledgment is made to the following publications in which several of these poems first appeared: *The American Poetry Review, Brick, Five Points, The New York Review of Books, The New Yorker, Notre Dame Review, Ploughshares, Poetry, Poetry Review* (U.K.), *Selected Poems* (U.K.), and *The Yale Review*.

Copper Canyon Press is in residence at Fort Worden State Park in Port Townsend, Washington, under the auspices of Centrum. Centrum is a gathering place for artists and creative thinkers from around the world, students of all ages and backgrounds, and audiences seeking extraordinary cultural enrichment.

The Library of Congress has cataloged the hardcover edition as follows:

LIBRARY OF CONGRESS CATALOGING-IN-PUBLICATION DATA

Merwin, W. S. (William Stanley), 1927–
The shadow of Sirius / W.S. Merwin.
    p.   cm.
Poems.
ISBN 978-1-55659-284-3 (hardcover: alk. paper)
1. Title.
PS3563.E75S48 2008
811'.54 — dc22

                                                                    2008014578

ISBN 978-1-55659-310-9

9 8 7 6 5 4 3 2 FIRST PRINTING

COPPER CANYON PRESS
Post Office Box 271
Port Townsend, Washington 98368
www.coppercanyonpress.org

to Paula

Contents

I

The Shadow of Sirius

I

The Nomad Flute

You that sang to me once sing to me now
let me hear your long lifted note
survive with me
the star is fading
I can think farther than that but I forget
do you hear me

do you still hear me
does your air
remember you
o breath of morning
night song morning song
I have with me
all that I do not know
I have lost none of it

but I know better now
than to ask you
where you learned that music
where any of it came from
once there were lions in China

I will listen until the flute stops
and the light is old again

Blueberries After Dark

So this is the way the night tastes
one at a time
not early or late

my mother told me
that I was not afraid of the dark
and when I looked it was true

how did she know
so long ago

with her father dead
almost before she could remember
and her mother following him
not long after
and then her grandmother
who had brought her up
and a little later
her only brother
and then her firstborn
gone as soon
as he was born
she knew

Still Morning

It appears now that there is only one
age and it knows
nothing of age as the flying birds know
nothing of the air they are flying through
or of the day that bears them up
through themselves
and I am a child before there are words
arms are holding me up in a shadow
voices murmur in a shadow
as I watch one patch of sunlight moving
across the green carpet
in a building
gone long ago and all the voices
silent and each word they said in that time
silent now
while I go on seeing that patch of sunlight

By the Avenue

Through the trees and across the river
with its surface the color of steel
on a rainy morning late in spring
the splintered skyline of the city
glitters in a silence we all know
but cannot touch or reach for with words
and I am the only one who can
remember now over there among
the young leaves brighter than the daylight
another light through the tall windows
a sunbeam sloping like a staircase
and from beyond it my father's voice
telling about a mote in an eye
that was like a mote in a sunbeam

Note

Remember how the naked soul
comes to language and at once knows
loss and distance and believing

then for a time it will not run
with its old freedom
like a light innocent of measure
but will hearken to how
one story becomes another
and will try to tell where
they have emerged from
and where they are heading
as though they were its own legend
running before the words and beyond them
naked and never looking back

through the noise of questions

Accompaniment

The wall in front of me is all one black
mirror in which I see my hands
washing themselves all by themselves
knowing what they are doing
as though they belong to someone
I do not see there and have never seen
who must be older than I am
since he knows what he is doing
above the basin of bright metal
in the black wall where the water looks
still as a frozen lake at night
though the bright ripples on it
are trembling and under me the floor
and my feet on it are trembling
it is late it was late when we started
over my shoulder my mother's voice
is telling me what we do next
on the way and how the train is made
that is taking us away and in a while
I will be asleep and I will
wake up far away
we are going south
where I know that my father
is going to die
but I will grow up before he does that
the hands go on washing by themselves

Without Knowing

If we could fly would there be numbers
apart from the seasons
in sleep I was flying south
so it was autumn
numberless autumn with its leaves
already far below me
some were falling into
the river of day
the invisible surface
that remembers and whispers
but does not tell even in sleep
not this time

The Song of the Trolleys

It was one of the carols
of summer and I knew that
even when all the leaves
were falling through it as it passed
and when frost crusted the tracks
as soon as they had stopped ringing
summer stayed on in that song
going again the whole way
out of sight to the river
under the hill and hissing
when it had to stop
then humming to itself
while it waited until
it could start again
out of an echo warning
once more with a clang of its bell
I could hear it coming
from far summers that I
had never known
long before I could see it
swinging its head
to its own tune on its way
and hardly arrived before it
was going and its singing
receding with its growing
smaller until it was gone
into sounds that resound
only when they have come to silence
the voices of morning stars
and the notes that once rose
out of the throats of women

from cold mountain villages
at the fringe of the forest
calling over the melting
snow to the spirits asleep
in the green heart of the woods
Wake now it is time again

From the Start

Who did I think was listening
when I wrote down the words
in pencil at the beginning
words for singing
to music I did not know
and people I did not know
would read them and stand to sing them
already knowing them
while they sing they have no names

Far Along in the Story

The boy walked on with a flock of cranes
following him calling as they came
from the horizon behind him
sometimes he thought he could recognize
a voice in all that calling but he
could not hear what they were calling
and when he looked back he could not tell
one of them from another in their
rising and falling but he went on
trying to remember something in
their calls until he stumbled and came
to himself with the day before him
wide open and the stones of the path
lying still and each tree in its own leaves
the cranes were gone from the sky and at
that moment he remembered who he was
only he had forgotten his name

The Pinnacle

Both of us understood
what a privilege it was
to be out for a walk
with each other
we could tell from our different
heights that this
kind of thing happened
so rarely that it might
not come round again
for me to be allowed
even before I
had started school
to go out for a walk
with Miss Giles
who had just retired
from being a teacher all her life

she was beautiful
in her camel hair coat
that seemed like the autumn leaves
our walk was her idea
we liked listening to each other
her voice was soft and sure
and we went our favorite way
the first time just in case
it was the only time
even though it might be too far
we went all the way
up the Palisades to the place
we called the pinnacle
with its park at the cliff's edge

overlooking the river
it was already a secret
the pinnacle
as we were walking back
when the time was later
than we had realized
and in fact no one
seemed to know where we had been
even when she told them
no one had heard of the pinnacle

and then where did she go

Child Light

On through the darkening of the seeds and the bronze equinox
I remember the brightness of days in summer
too many years ago now to be counted
the cotton-white glare floating over the leaves
I see that it was only the dust in one sunbeam
but I was a child at the time

I hear our feet crossing the porch
and then the glass door opening
before we are conducted through the empty rooms of the house
where we are to live

that was on a day before I was nine
before the lake and the water sloshing in the boat
and what we heard about refugees
and before Billy Green explained to me about sex
and I saw my first strip mine
and before the war
and before the sound of the train wheels under me
when the leaves were still green
before the word for autumn

that was before Ching and Gypsy
and the sun on the kitchen table
with the window open
before the deaths by bombing
and by sickness and age and by fire and by gas
and by torture
and before the scratched varnish of the study hall
and before the camps
and coming to Conrad and Tolstoy

it was before the deaths of schoolchildren
whom I had known and whom I heard of

and before looking out into the trees after dark
from the window of the splintery unlit chemistry lab
into the scent of the first fallen leaves

Empty Lot

There was only the narrow alley between us
and we lived beside the long dusty patch
of high ragweed that first parched summer
and then the heart leaves of the old poplar cradled
down to the dust in the fall when the men gathered there
of an evening to toss quoits into the sky
toward the clay pits facing them and in winter
the drifted snow showed where the wind whirled
between the houses and I watched the sun go down
out beyond there behind the mountain
and the moon sailing over the lot late at night
when I woke out of a dream of flying
and yet there was no way to imagine that place
as it had been for so long
with the world to itself before there were houses
when bears took their time there under trees they knew
now we were told that it belonged to
the D&H Coal Company and they
would do nothing with it but keep it
in case they ever should need to sink
an emergency shaft to miners
in trouble below there nobody could say
how far down but sometimes when the night
was utterly still we knew we had just heard
the muffled thump of a blast under us
and the house knew it the windows trembled
we listened for picks ticking in the dark

No

Out at the end of the street in the cemetery
the tombstones stared across the wheeling shadows
of tombstones while the names and dates wept on
in full daylight and behind them where the hill
sheared off two rusted tracks under a black
iron gate led up out of pure darkness
and the unbroken sound of pure darkness
that went on all the time under everything
not breathing beneath the sounds of breathing
but no they said it was not the entrance
to the underworld or anything like that
in fact all the houses along the street
had been paid for by what had come from there
in the days of the negatives of the pictures

The Piano

It may have survived to this day somewhere
in another life
where they speak of its age as a measure of unimportance
not realizing that it was always as old as it is now
something I understand from its sound which has not changed
coming from the slender valleys under the keys
never explored and not expecting to be noticed

each valley waking a different echo
out of the narrow vibrant shadow
between the piano and the wall that emerges above it
papered to be wheat fields without wind
with no horizon and with a smell of walls and night

through the notes my mother's hand appears
above my own and hovers over the keys
waiting to turn the pages of Czerny
whose composition has completely dissolved

from her hand a scent of almonds rises
which she had put on after whatever she had been doing
it survives with the sound into another life

some time ago a few inches of beaded molding
fell from the panel behind the music rack
to lie at the foot of it waiting to be put back

her fingers remember the right notes and keep listening for them
the veins on the backs of her hands are the color
of the clear morning sky beginning to haze over

Secrets

Time unseen time our continuing fiction
however we tell it eludes our dear hope and our reason

that is a pure condition of the story
and wherever our parents came from is another century

an age which they themselves could barely remember
but carried with them as their own year after year

hidden away hardly looked at until the secret
without their noticing had faded all the details white

for my mother it came to be the lace veil covering
the front of the baby carriage where she was being

wheeled through the Garden of the Gods when her parents were
still alive as she told about it later

and for my father it was the glare bleaching the surface
of the river as he sat under the white blaze

of summer in the rowboat tied above the waterline
where he was allowed to hold the oars and imagine

leaving did he see any farther when he was
dying in summer after midnight and before the solstice

coughing saying he was not afraid and was the veil still there
when my mother turned from her own garden one evening that same year

telling a friend on the telephone that she was going
to get some rest now and her glasses were lying

apart from her on the floor not more than an hour
later when a neighbor pushed the door open and found her

A Likeness

Almost to your birthday and as I
am getting dressed alone in the house
a button comes off and once I find
a needle with an eye big enough
for me to try to thread it
and at last have sewed the button on
I open an old picture of you
who always did such things by magic
one photograph found after you died
of you at twenty
beautiful in a way
I would never see
for that was nine years
before I was born
but the picture has
faded suddenly
spots have marred it
maybe it is past repair
I have only what I remember

Raiment

Believing comes after
there were coverings
who can believe
that we were born without them
he she or it wailing
back the first breath
from a stark reflection
raw and upside-down
early but already
not original

into the last days
and then some way past them
the body that we
are assured is more
than what covers it
is kept covered
out of habit which
is a word for dress
out of custom
which is an alteration
of the older word *costume*
out of decency
which is handed down
from a word for what
is fitting

apparently we believe
in the words
and through them
but we long beyond them

for what is unseen
what remains out of reach
what is kept covered
with colors and sizes
we hunger
for what is undoubted yet dubious
known to be different
and our fabrics tell
of difference
we dress in difference
calling it ours

Europe

After days untold the word
comes You will see it
tomorrow you will
see what you have only heard of
ever since you were too small
to understand And that night
which I would scarcely remember
I lay looking up through
the throb of iron at sea
trying again to remember
how I believed it would look
and in the morning light
from the bow of the freighter
that I know must have gone by now
to the breaker's decades ago
I could make out the shadow
on the horizon before us
that was the coast of Spain
and as we came closer another
low shape passing before it
like a hand on a dial
a warship I recognized
from a model of it I had made
when I was a child
and beyond it
there was a road down the cliff
that I would descend some years later
and recognize it
there we were all together
one time

Photographer

Later in the day
after he had died and the long box
full of shadow had turned the corner
and perhaps he no longer was watching
what the light was doing
as its white blaze climbed higher
bleaching the street and drying the depths
to a blank surface

when they started to excavate the burrow
under the roof where he had garnered his life
and to drag it all out into the raw moment
and carry it down the stairs
armload by armload to the waiting dumpcart
nests of bedding clothes from their own days
shards of the kitchen there were a few bundled papers
and stacks of glass plates heavy and sliding
easily broken before they could be got down
to the tumbril and mule
pieces grinding underfoot
all over the floor and down the stairs
as they would remember

fortunately someone who understood
what was on the panes bought everything in the studio
almost no letters were there but on the glass
they turned up face after face
of the light before anyone had beheld it
there were its cobbled lanes leading far into themselves
apple trees flowering in another century
lilies open in sunlight against former house walls

worn flights of stone stairs before the war
in days not seen except by the bent figure
invisible under the hood
who had just disappeared

Traces

Papers already darkened
deckled because of the many years
bear signs of a sole moment
of someone's passage
that surely was mine
not a sound of it now
coming from its land
that was all there was
in its time
with all its leaves
and the barking not noticed
in the distance
and the silence in the books then

now the machine that does that
is taking the world away
just across the streambed
at the foot of the garden
what can abide as we
follow among those
who have forgotten
and what do we remember
eyes but not the seeing
often we did not know
that we were happy
even when we were not
how could we have known that
at no distance

Inheritance

At my elbow on the table
it lies open as it has done
for a good part of these thirty
years ever since my father died
and it passed into my hands
this *Webster's New International*
Dictionary of the English
Language of 1922
on India paper which I
was always forbidden to touch
for fear I would tear or somehow
damage its delicate pages
heavy in their binding
this color of wet sand
on which thin waves hover
when it was printed he was twenty-six
they had not been married four years
he was a country preacher
in a one-store town and I suppose
a man came to the door one day
peddling this new dictionary
on fine paper like the Bible
at an unrepeatable price
and it seemed it would represent
a distinction just to own it
confirming something about him
that he could not even name
now its cover is worn as though
it had been carried on journeys
across the mountains and deserts
of the earth but it has been here

beside me the whole time
what has frayed it like that
loosening it gnawing at it
all through these years
I know I must have used it
much more than he did but always
with care and indeed affection
turning the pages patiently
in search of meanings

A Broken Glass

Gold rim worn bare here and there

gold ring below it
broken after more than two centuries
nine facets under it tapering inward
suddenly splintered with a new light
irrevocable as light is
while the stem on which they converge
with six facets flowing down it
remains untouched
and the base onto which they run out
like streams frozen below their waterfalls
has noticed nothing heard nothing
and it is only when the glass has been broken
after holding so many days and nights
that I see clearly on the pieces the whole flower
the tall gold iris that has been growing there
longer than I know

out of the gold ground

Lament for a Stone

The bay where I found you faced the long light
of the west glowing under the cold sky

there Columba as the story goes looked
back and could not see Ireland any more

therefore he could stay he made up his mind
in that slur of the sea on the shingle

shaped in a fan around the broad crescent
formed all of green pebbles found nowhere else

flecked with red held in blue depths and polished
smooth as water by rolling like water

along each other rocking as they were
rocking at his feet it is said that they

are proof against drowning and I saw you
had the shape of the long heart of a bird

and when I took you in my palm we flew
through the years hearing them rush under us

where have you flown now leaving me to hear
that sound alone without you in my hand

A Note from the Cimmerians

By the time it gets to us
we can make nothing of it
but questions or else it makes
us turn out to be only
questions that we are helpless
not to ask
in the first place
is it real which is to say
is it authentic which is
to say is it from someone
not one of us and if so
how do we know that and where
has it come from what petal
of our compass or from what
age of the orbiting phrase
before us as we say it
in the language we speak now
and for whom was it set down
or to whom is it addressed
now or will it speak later
in another meaning and
is it a question itself
or the back of a question
advancing or receding
from our point of view and are
we to believe they exist
in truth those shapes of antique
hearsay whom no one has seen
by day the Cimmerians
who dwell in utter darkness
it is said or perhaps live
on the other side of it

A Codex

It was a late book given up for lost
again and again with its sentences

bare at last and phrases that seemed transparent
revealing what had been there the whole way

the poems of daylight after the day
lying open at last on the table

without explanation or emphasis
like sounds left when the syllables have gone

clarifying the whole grammar of waiting
not removing one question from the air

or closing the story although single lights
were beginning by then above and below

while the long twilight deepened its silence
from sapphire through opal to Athena's iris

until shadow covered the gray pages
the comet words the book of presences

after which there was little left to say
but then it was night and everything was known

Beyond Question

What is it then
that Kent said he could see
in Lear's countenance
he called it authority
to give it a name
though it is recognized
whenever seen or heard
whether it is staring
from the pupil
of the dead animal
or blocking the road
when the brakes have gone
or irreversible
in the doctor's syllables
or in the headline or the fine
print or the waiting envelope
or surfacing in the mirror
it is there
whole untouched never
answering it is in
the sound of breathing
and in a voice
bird or human calling calling
it burns in the single
instant of pain
flashing its colors
it runs in the mind
of water and in
the dumbness of touch
in the only light
in the pace of nightfall

Youth

Through all of youth I was looking for you
without knowing what I was looking for

or what to call you I think I did not
even know I was looking how would I

have known you when I saw you as I did
time after time when you appeared to me

as you did naked offering yourself
entirely at that moment and you let

me breathe you touch you taste you knowing
no more than I did and only when I

began to think of losing you did I
recognize you when you were already

part memory part distance remaining
mine in the ways that I learn to miss you

from what we cannot hold the stars are made

II

in memory of Muku, Makana, Koa

By Dark

When it is time I follow the black dog
into the darkness that is the mind of day

I can see nothing there but the black dog
the dog I know going ahead of me

not looking back oh it is the black dog
I trust now in my turn after the years

when I had all the trust of the black dog
through an age of brightness and through shadow

on into the blindness of the black dog
where the rooms of the dark were already known

and had no fear in them for the black dog
leading me carefully up the blind stairs

Calling a Distant Animal

Here it is once again this one note
from a string of longing

tightened suddenly from both ends
and held for plucking

tone torn out of one birdsong
though that bird

by now may be
where a call cannot

follow it
the same note goes on calling

across space and is heard now
in the old night and known there

a silence recognized
by the silence it calls to

Night with No Moon

Now you are darker than I can believe
it is not wisdom that I have come to

with its denials and pure promises
but this absence that I cannot set down

still hearing when there is nothing to hear
reaching into the blindness that was there

thinking to walk in the dark together

Good Night

Sleep softly my old love
my beauty in the dark
night is a dream we have
as you know as you know

night is a dream you know
an old love in the dark
around you as you go
without end as you know

in the night where you go
sleep softly my old love
without end in the dark
in the love that you know

At the Bend

I look for you my curl of sleep
my breathing wave on the night shore
my star in the fog of morning
I think you can always find me

I call to you under my breath
I whisper to you through the hours
all your names my ear of shadow
I think you can always hear me

I wait for you my promised day
my time again my homecoming
my being where you wait for me
I think always of you waiting

Into the Cloud

What do you have with you
now my small traveller
suddenly on the way
and all at once so far

on legs that never were
up to the life that you
led them and breathing with
the shortness breath comes to

my endless company
when you could come to me
you would stay close to me
until the day was done

o closest to my breath
if you are able to
please wait a while longer
on that side of the cloud

Another Dream of Burial

Sometimes it is a walled garden
with the stone over the entrance
broken and inside it a few
silent dried-up weeds or it may
be a long pool perfectly still
with the clear water revealing
no color but that of the gray
stone around it and once there was
in a painting of a landscape
one torn place imperfectly mended
that showed the darkness under it
but still I have set nothing down
and turned and walked away from it
into the whole world

A Ring

At this moment
this earth which for all we know

is the only place in the vault of darkness
with life on it is wound in a fine veil

of whispered voices groping the frayed waves
of absence they keep flaring up

out of hope entwined with its opposite
to wander in ignorance as we do

when we look for what we have lost
one moment touching the earth and the next

straying far out past the orbits and webs
and the static of knowledge they go on

without being able to tell whether
they are addressing the past or the future

or knowing where they are heard these words
of the living talking to the dead

Little Soul

*after Hadrian**

Little soul little stray
little drifter
now where will you stay
all pale and all alone
after the way
you used to make fun of things

*See page 114

Trail Marker

One white tern sails calling
across the evening sky
under the few high clouds touched
with the first flush of sunset
while the tide keeps going out
going out to the south
all day it has been six months
that you have been gone
and then the tern is gone
and only the clouds are there
and the sounds of the late tide

Dream of Koa Returning

Sitting on the steps of that cabin
that I had always known
with its porch and gray-painted floorboards
I looked out to the river
flowing beyond the big trees
and all at once you
were just behind me
lying watching me
as you did years ago
and not stirring at all
when I reached back slowly
hoping to touch
your long amber fur
and there we stayed without moving
listening to the river
and I wondered whether
it might be a dream
whether you might be a dream
whether we both were a dream
in which neither of us moved

III

Cargo

The moment at evening
when the pictures set sail from the walls
with their lights out
unmooring without hesitation or stars
they carry no questions
as their unseen sails
the beginning and the end
wing and wing
bear them out beyond
the faces each set in its instant
and beyond the landscapes of other times
and the tables piled with fruit
just picked and with motionless
animals all together known
in the light as still lives
they sail on the sound of night
bearing with them that life
they have been trying to show
from dawn until dark

Going

Only humans believe
there is a word for goodbye
we have one in every language
one of the first words we learn
it is made out of greeting
but they are going away
the raised hand waving
the face the person the place
the animal the day
leaving the word behind
and what it was meant to say

The Curlew

When the moon has gone I fly on alone
into this night where I have never been

the eggshell of dark before and after
in its height I am older and younger

than all that I have come to and beheld
and carry still untouched across the cold

Nocturne

The stars emerge one
by one into the names
that were last found for them
far back in other
darkness no one remembers
by watchers whose own
names were forgotten
later in the dark
and as the night deepens
other lumens begin
to appear around them
as though they were shining
through the same instant
from a single depth of age
though the time between
each one of them
and its nearest neighbor
contains in its span
the whole moment of the earth
turning in a light
that is not its own
with the complete course
of life upon it
born to brief reflection
recognition and anguish
from one cell evolving
to remember daylight
laughter and distant music

Day without a Name

Not today then
will it be here after all
the word for this time
the name its age
today nothing is missing
except the word for it
the morning is too
beautiful to be anything else
too brief for waiting
and behind its pellucid passage
another light that does not
appear to be moving
fills the horizon
there the word
waited for
like a wild creature
not glimpsed this season
not seen by anyone
must be watching

Recognitions

Stories come to us like new senses

a wave and an ash tree were sisters
they had been separated since they were children
but they went on believing in each other
though each was sure that the other must be lost
they cherished traits of themselves that they thought of
as family resemblances features they held in common
the sheen of the wave fluttered in remembrance
of the undersides of the leaves of the ash tree
in summer air and the limbs of the ash tree
recalled the wave as the breeze lifted it
and they wrote to each other every day
without knowing where to send the letters
some of which have come to light only now
revealing in their old but familiar language
a view of the world we could not have guessed at

but that we always wanted to believe

Escape Artist

When they arrange the cages
for experiments
they have long known
that there is no magic
in foxes at any time
singly or by species
color region gender
whether in the wild
or after generations
bred in captivity
for some grade of fur
or trait of character
for the benefit
of a distant
inquiring relative
living in ambush and hope
clothes and mourning

but what after all
was magic and where
could it have come from
as the experts considered this
wordless descendant
of countless visions
apparitions tales
that vanished in the telling
this heir of conjurers
of disappearing acts
caged now in numbers
lost in plain sight

The Mole

Here is yet one
more life that we see only from outside
from the outside

not in itself but later
in signs of its going
a reminder
in the spring daylight

it happened when we were not noticing
and so close to us
that we might not have been here
disregarded as we were

see where we have walked
the earth has risen again
out of its darkness
where it has been recognized
without being seen
known by touch
of the blind velvet fingers
the wise nails
descendants of roots and water

we have seen them
only in death and in pictures
opened from darkness afterward

but here the earth
has been touched and raised
eye has not seen it come

ear has not heard
the famous fur
the moment that finds its way
in the dark without us

Eye of Shadow

Sentry of the other side
it may have watched the beginning
without being noticed in all
that blossoming radiance
the beggar in dark rags
down on the dark threshold
a shadow waiting

in its own fair time
all in its rags it rises
revealing its prime claim
upon the latter day
that fades around it
while the sky is turning
with the whole prophecy

o lengthening dark vision
reaching across faces
across colors and mountains
and all that is known
or appears to be known
herald without a sound
leave-taking without a word
guide beyond time and knowledge
o patience
beyond patience

I touch the day
I taste the light
I remember

A Letter to Ruth Stone

Now that you have caught sight
of the other side of darkness
the invisible side
so that you can tell
it is rising
first thing in the morning
and know it is there
all through the day

another sky
clear and unseen
has begun to loom
in your words
and another light is growing
out of their shadows
you can hear it

now you will be able
to envisage beyond
any words of mine
the color of these leaves
that you never saw
awake above the still valley
in the small hours
under the moon
three nights past the full

you know there was never
a name for that color

Worn Words

The late poems are the ones
I turn to first now
following a hope that keeps
beckoning me
waiting somewhere in the lines
almost in plain sight

it is the late poems
that are made of words
that have come the whole way
they have been there

A Letter to Su Tung-p'o

Almost a thousand years later
I am asking the same questions
you did the ones you kept finding
yourself returning to as though
nothing had changed except the tone
of their echo growing deeper
and what you knew of the coming
of age before you had grown old
I do not know any more now
than you did then about what you
were asking as I sit at night
above the hushed valley thinking
of you on your river that one
bright sheet of moonlight in the dream
of the waterbirds and I hear
the silence after your questions
how old are the questions tonight

Bashō's Child

Beside the Fuji River
there is a lost child crying
dead for three hundred years
and who knows how many more
since the evening in autumn
when her mother carried her
out to the water noise
that would cover the sound of her crying
and then walked back into the silence
and the child cried all night
and into the frosty daylight
when the men who discovered her
stood over her like shadows
their hands talking but only
to each other until one of them
at last bent to put something
on the leaves beside her
before they all went away
with the sound of her crying
following him and following
the words he would write about her
wherever the words might go

The Odds

His first winter in that city
after years in the north a friend
wrote to me of how people there
were dealing with the cold
he told me that crews
were digging up the avenue
down at the corner all day
the men keeping a fire going
in an old oil drum with holes
down the sides and feeding it whatever
turned up and he had been watching
two men by the barrel with three
gloves between them passing one
glove back and forth
while they stamped their feet
and he had tried to tell whether
it was a right or a left glove

The Long and the Short of It

As long as we can believe anything
we believe in measure
we do it with the first breath we take
and the first sound we make
it is in each word we learn
and in each of them it means
what will come again and when
it is there in *meal* and in *moon*
and in *meaning* it is the meaning
it is the firmament and the furrow
turning at the end of the field
and the verse turning with its breath
it is in memory that keeps telling us
some of the old story about us

Unknown Age

For all the features it hoards and displays
age seems to be without substance at any time

whether morning or evening it is a moment of air
held between the hands like a stunned bird

while I stand remembering light in the trees
of another century on a continent long submerged

with no way of telling whether the leaves at that time
felt memory as they were touching the day

and no knowledge of what happened to the reflections
on the pond's surface that never were seen again

the bird lies still while the light goes on flying

My Hand

See how the past is not finished
here in the present
it is awake the whole time
never waiting
it is my hand now but not what I held
it is not my hand but what I held
it is what I remember
but it never seems quite the same
no one else remembers it
a house long gone into air
the flutter of tires over a brick road
cool light in a vanished bedroom
the flash of the oriole
between one life and another
the river a child watched

What the Bridges Hear

Even the right words if ever
we come to them tell of something
the words never knew
celestia for starlight
or *starlight* for starlight
so at this moment there may be words
somewhere among the nebulae
for the two bridges across the wide
rock-strewn river
part way around the bend from each other
in the winter sunlight
late in the afternoon more than half
a century ago with the sound
of the water rushing under them
and passing between them unvarying
and inaudible it is still there
so is the late sunlight
of that winter afternoon
although the winter has vanished
and the bridges are still reaching across
the wide sound of being there

The First Days

As I come from a continent
that I saw closing behind me
like a lost element
day after day before
I believed I was leaving it

here surfacing through the long
backlight of my recollection
is this other world veiled
in its illusion of being known
at the moment of daybreak
when the dreams all at once are gone
into shadow leaving only
in their place the familiar
once-familiar landscape

with its road open to the south
the roofs emerging on the way
from their own orbits according
to an order as certain
as the seasons
the fields emerald and mustard
and beyond them the precession
of hills with red cows on the slopes
and then the edging clouds of sheep

and the house door at evening
one old verb in the lock turning
and the fragrance of cold stone as once more
the door cedes in a dark hush
that neither answers nor forgets
and an unchanged astonishment

that has never been tamed nor named
nor held in the hand
nor ever fully seen
but it is still the same
a vision before news a gift
of flight in a dream
of clear depths where I glimpse
far out of reach the lucent days
from which now I am made

Heartland

From the beginning it belonged to distance
as the blue color of the mountain does

and though it existed on a map somewhere
and might be discovered by chance
and even be recognized perhaps
at an odd moment

it survived beyond
what could be known at the time
in its archaic
untaught language
that brings the bees to the rosemary

many years after it had been found
its true name remained
on the other side of knowledge

yet it was still there
like a season that has changed
but appears in the light

in the unspoken morning

Long Afternoon Light

Small roads written in sleep in the foothills
how long ago and I believed you were lost
with the bronze then deepening in the light
and the shy moss turning to itself holding
its own brightness above the badger's path
while a single crow sailed west without a sound
we trust without giving it a thought
that we will always see it as we see it
once and that what we know is only
a moment of what is ours and will stay
we believe it as the moment slips away
as lengthening shadows merge in the valley
and a window kindles there like a first star
what we see again comes to us in secret

Cave

Stone room dug into the brow of the ridge
one corner of it the rose-gray living rock
that covers the dark halls of the underworld
great maned green water-dog on the south wall
where the whitewash is mottled to a map of time
casement windows to the north facing
the quilt of small fields and the bend of river
far below them and set into the hillside
in the east wall the ancient oven mouth
a dark shape like the backs of sunrise and moonrise
and the black arches of the woodstove with its scrolls
of iron leaves and love goddess and rainbow
I have come back through the years to this
stone hollow encrypted in its own stillness
I hear it without listening

The Morning Hills

As those who are gone now
keep wandering through our words
sounds of paper following them
at untold distances
so I wake again in the old house
where at times I have believed
that I was waiting for myself
and many years have gone
taking with them the semblance of youth
reason after reason ranges of blue hills
who did I think was missing
those days neither here nor there
my own dog waiting
to be known

Cold Spring Morning

At times it has seemed that when
I first came here it was an old self
I recognized in the silent walls
and the river far below
but the self has no age
as I knew even then and had known
for longer than I could remember
as the sky has no sky
except itself this white morning in May
with fog hiding the barns
that are empty now and hiding the mossed
limbs of gnarled walnut trees and the green
pastures unfurled along the slope
I know where they are and the birds
that are hidden in their own calls
in the cold morning
I was not born here I come and go

Near Field

This is not something new or kept secret
the tilled ground unsown in late spring
the dead are not separate from the living
each has one foot in the unknown
and cannot speak for the other
the field tells none of its turned story
it lies under its low cloud like a waiting river
the dead made this out of their hunger
out of what they had been told
out of the pains and shadows
and bowels of animals
out of turning and
coming back singing
about another time

To Paula in Late Spring

Let me imagine that we will come again
when we want to and it will be spring
we will be no older than we ever were
the worn griefs will have eased like the early cloud
through which the morning slowly comes to itself
and the ancient defenses against the dead
will be done with and left to the dead at last
the light will be as it is now in the garden
that we have made here these years together
of our long evenings and astonishment

Youth of Grass

Yesterday in the hushed white sunlight
down along the meadows by the river
through all the bright hours they cut the first hay
of this year to leave it tossed in long rows
leading into the twilight and long evening
while thunderheads grumbled from the horizon
and now the whole valley and the slopes around it
that look down to the sky in the river
are fragrant with hay as this night comes in
and the owl cries across the new spaces
to the mice suddenly missing their sky
and so the youth of this spring all at once is over
it has come upon us again taking us
once more by surprise just as we began
to believe that those fields would always be green

The Silence of the Mine Canaries

The bats have not flowered
for years now in the crevice
of the tower wall when the long twilight
of spring has seeped across it
as the west light brought back
the colors of parting
the furred buds have not hung there
waking among their dark petals
before sailing out blind along their own echoes
whose high infallible cadenzas only
they could hear completely and could ride
to take over at that hour
from the swallows gliding
ever since daybreak over the garden
from their nests under the eaves
skimming above the house and the hillside pastures
their voices glittering in their exalted tongue
who knows how long now since they have been seen
and the robins have gone from the barn
where the cows spent the summer days
though they stayed long after the cows were gone
the flocks of five kinds of tits have not come again
the blue tits that nested each year
in the wall where their young
could be heard deep in the stones by the window
calling *Here Here* have not returned
the marks of their feet are still there on the stone
of their doorsill that does not know
what it is missing
the cuckoo has not been heard
again this May

nor for many a year the nightjar
nor the mistle thrush song thrush whitethroat
the blackcap that instructed Mendelssohn
I have seen them
I have stood and listened
I was young
they were singing of youth
not knowing that they were singing for us

Walled Place above the River

There are fields smaller than this
I have seen them tilled and harvested
by the old who still labored by hand
down the lane and out on the upland
where they are forgotten now
their own names do not believe in them

and there are rooms bigger than this
in houses I have visited
finding myself in occasions
full of voices or sometimes silence
but not the silence here

the lid of earth inside the walls
in Dublin where Hopkins' bones were left
among those of fellow Jesuits
as I recall it is of a size
roughly comparable to this
which years ago I thought might be
where my own remains should lie

over there in the northeast corner
under the oak with the whole valley
beyond it blue at noon and the voice
of the oriole tumbling
from the woods to the east again
after years of absence
and three black-and-orange butterflies
cruising the white glare of the grass
is the only grave I know here

that of the donkey abandoned
by his mother and carried to the barn
cold nose out of the brambles
into which he had rolled and he followed
us and the warm bottle for a week
this is not a place made for knowledge

I do not know what the enclosure was built for
dug out facing north
toward the far side of the river
and levelled like a terrace
and why the walls were raised
stone on stone to form a square
with the two narrow passages
one toward the barn one toward the fields below
nor who made it nor how long ago

but I have been listening to it
since I was young and its voice is the same
though the leaves have changed and the seasons
and some of the longings
now a soft breath stirs the trees as morning ends
in a few days it will be summer

A Horse Heaven

The fence is new and the gate in it
of the same thin green wire that is there
just to remind them that they are home
in the long pasture below the woods
the tall gray horses all slender mares
moving lightly as clouds before me
close to me curious none of them
can remember me I tell myself
all of them must have been born since I
was here last and some of the young ones
watch me over their shoulders taking
no chances but some of the elders
move near to me with the same small wave
nudging them on and they look at me
as though maybe they had once known me

One of the Butterflies

The trouble with pleasure is the timing
it can overtake me without warning
and be gone before I know it is here
it can stand facing me unrecognized
while I am remembering somewhere else
in another age or someone not seen
for years and never to be seen again
in this world and it seems that I cherish
only now a joy I was not aware of
when it was here although it remains
out of reach and will not be caught or named
or called back and if I could make it stay
as I want to it would turn into pain

Parts of a Tune

One old man keeps humming the same few notes
of some song he thought he had forgotten
back in the days when as he knows there was
no word for *life* in the language
and if they wanted to say *eyes* or *heart*
they would hold up a leaf and he remembers
the big tree where it rose from the dry ground
and the way the birds carried water in their voices
they were all the color of their fear of the dark
and as he sits there humming he remembers
some of the words they come back to him now
he smiles hearing them come and go

Nocturne II

August arrives in the dark

we are not even asleep and it is here
with a gust of rain rustling before it
how can it be so late all at once
somewhere the Perseids are falling
toward us already at a speed that would
burn us alive if we could believe it
but in the stillness after the rain ends
nothing is to be heard but the drops falling
one at a time from the tips of the leaves
into the night and I lie in the dark
listening to what I remember
while the night flies on with us into itself

White Note

Autumn comes early this year
the last morning of August
fog fills the valley clouding
the late roses and the scent
of wet leaves floats in the light
one day after the full moon
it is the time of going
small flocks of migrant birds catch
like strands of wool in the trees
west of the village and wait
for something to remind them
of the journey and their own
way and when the fog lifts
they have gone and with them the days
of summer have vanished
and the leaves here and there begin
taking to themselves
the colors of sunlight
to keep them

Gray Herons in the Field above the River

Now that the nights turn longer than the days
we are standing in the still light after dawn

in the high grass of autumn that is green again
hushed in its own place after the burn of summer

each of us stationed alone without moving
at a perfect distance from all the others

like shadows of ourselves risen out of our shadows
each eye without turning continues to behold

what is moving
each of us is one of seven now

we have come a long way sailing our opened clouds
remembering all night where the world would be

the clear shallow stream the leaves floating along it
the dew in the hushed field the only morning

No Shadow

Dog grief and the love of coffee
lengthen like a shadow of mine

and now that my eyes no longer
swear to anything I look out

through the cloud light of this autumn
and see the valley where I came

first more than half my life ago
oh more than half with its river

a sky in the palm of a hand
never unknown and never known

never mine and never not mine
beyond it into the distance

the ridges reflect the clouds now
through a morning without shadows

the river still seems not to move
as though it were the same river

The Making of Amber

The September flocks form crying
gathering southward
even small birds knowing
for the first time
how to fly all the way as one

at daybreak the split fig
is filled with dew
the finch finds it
like something it remembers

then across the afternoon
the grape vine hangs low in the doorway
and grapes one by one
taste warm to the tongue
transparent and soundless
rich with late daylight

September's Child

September light gray and rose touches the ridge above the valley
seeps upward at daybreak through its own silence
without beginning without stages with white clouds still cloaking the river
and a great ship of towers anchored on the one hill that rises through them
then amber morning and the markets unfolding
smiles of veteran vendors assembled once more in bright day
old hands holding honey jars sunlight on weathered faces
knowing summer and winter well but bound to neither of them
in the cool fragrance of wild strawberries raspberries spice bread
a morning when the first green figs are ripening
and single birds come bringing their late hopes as the light warms
recognizing through the remaining leaves a moment they have never seen
as I do waking again here after many lifetimes
to the sight of a morning before I was born

Remembering the Wings

What became of all the pigeons
along the ridge of the barn roof
the crest on the dark red tiled slope
those black Mondains broad as barges
the pheasant wings of the Cauchoises
the brilliant buffed copper Bouvreuils
the Carneauxs forever fighting
both Montaubans trailing their grace
elegant and amiable
two long indolent innocents
easy-come Bertie and Midnight
crown princes born for fair weather
Édouard said the fox would get them
Verdun still not far in his mind
out there watching in the long grass
it would climb up like a shadow
then what became of the children
who had gone to school with him
in the house just beyond the barn
even then the war was lying
out in the summer fields waiting
and then what became of Édouard
when I look and the roof is bare

Shadow Hand

Duporte the roofer that calm voice
those sure hands gentling weathered tiles
into new generations or
half of him rising through a roof
like some sea spirit from a wave
to turn shaped slates into fish scales
that would swim in the rain Duporte
who seemed to smooth arguments by
listening and whom they sent for
when a bone was broken or when
they had a pig to kill because
of the way he did it only
yesterday after all these years
I learned that he had suddenly
gone blind while still in his sixties
and died soon after that while I
was away and I never knew
and it seemed as though it had just
happened and it had not been long
since we stood in the road talking
about owls nesting in chimneys
in the dark in empty houses

Barrade

The stone tower on the barrens
alone there for five hundred years
grew back into night when night came
at its feet the walls around it
the dry pool the raised threshing floor
the ancient hollow acacia
the walnut trees by the pasture
were back in the dark they came from
the invisible sheep sifted
through sere grass with the circling sound
of a soft breath in the distance
later the owl the white lady
shrieked close across the darkened fields
to the mice waiting for her there
visible to no one but her
as she sailed up onto the stone
top of the tower and from it sang
Me Me to her moment and then
maybe silence until the hour
when a far-off echo began
from the earth and down under it
coming nearer an iron note
the night train through the cut before
the long turn down to the valley
and for only an instant through
a gap at the end of a dark field
the strip of yellow windows passed
like the days on a calendar
the long rays of their reflections
reaching across the naked earth
a moment and then never gone

Into October

These must be the colors of returning
the leaves darkened now but staying on
into the bronzed morning among the seed heads
and the dry stems and the umbers of October
the secret season that appears on its own
a recognition without a sound
long after the day when I stood in its light
out on the parched barrens beside a spring
all but hidden in a tangle of eglantine
and picked the bright berries made of that summer

Lights Out

The old grieving autumn goes on calling to its summer
the valley is calling to other valleys beyond the ridge
each star is roaring alone into darkness
there is not a sound in the whole night

Falling

Long before daybreak
none of the birds yet awake
rain comes down with the sound
of a huge wind rushing
through the valley trees
it comes down around us
all at the same time
and beyond it there is nothing
it falls without hearing itself
without knowing
there is anyone here
without seeing where it is
or where it is going
like a moment of great
happiness of our own
that we cannot remember
coasting with the lights off

Grace Note

It is at last any morning
not answering to a name
I wake before there is light
hearing once more that same
music without repetition
or beginning playing
away into itself
in silence like a wave
a unison in its own
key that I seem
to have heard before I
was listening but by the time
I hear it now it is gone
as when on a morning
alive with sunlight
almost at the year's end
a feathered breath a bird
flies in at the open window
then vanishes leaving me
believing what I do not see

One Valley

Once I thought I could find
where it began
but that never happened
though I went looking for it
time and again
cutting my way past
empty pools and dry waterfalls
where my dog ran straight up the stone
like an unmoored flame

it seemed that the beginning
could not be far then
as I went on through the trees
over the rocks toward the mountain
until I came out in the open
and saw no sign of it

where the roaring torrent
raced at one time
to carve farther down
those high walls in the stone
for the silence that I hear now
day and night on its way to the sea

The Old Trees on the Hill

When you were living
and it was later than we knew
there was an old orchard
far up on the hill behind the house
dark apple trees wrapped in moss
standing deep in thorn bushes and wild grape
cobwebs breathing between the branches
memory lingering in silence
the spring earth fragrant with other seasons
crows conferred in those boughs and sailed on
chickadees talked of the place as their own
there were still kinglets and bluebirds
and the nuthatch following the folded bark
the churr of one wren a dark shooting star
with all that each of them knew then
but whoever had planted those trees
straightening now and again over the spade
to stand looking out across the curled
gleaming valley to the far gray ridges
one autumn after the leaves had fallen
while the morning frost still slept in the hollows
had been buried somewhere far from there
and those who had known him and his family
were completely forgotten you told me
and you said you had never been up there
though it was a place where you
loved to watch the daylight changing
and we looked up and watched the daylight there

A Single Autumn

The year my parents died
one that summer one that fall
three months and three days apart
I moved into the house
where they had lived their last years
it had never been theirs
and was still theirs in that way
for a while

echoes in every room
without a sound
all the things that we
had never been able to say
I could not remember

doll collection
in a china cabinet
plates stacked on shelves
lace on drop-leaf tables
a dried branch of bittersweet
before a hall mirror
were all planning to wait

the glass doors of the house
remained closed
the days had turned cold
and out in the tall hickories
the blaze of autumn had begun
on its own

I could do anything

Lake Shore in Half Light

There is a question I want to ask
and I can't remember it
I keep trying to
I know it is the same question
it has always been
in fact I seem to know
almost everything about it
all that reminds me of it
leading me to the lake shore
at daybreak or twilight
and to whatever is standing
next to the question
as a body stands next to its shadow
but the question is not a shadow
if I knew who discovered
zero I might ask
what there was before

A Momentary Creed

I believe in the ordinary day
that is here at this moment and is me

I do not see it going its own way
but I never saw how it came to me

it extends beyond whatever I may
think I know and all that is real to me

it is the present that it bears away
where has it gone when it has gone from me

there is no place I know outside today
except for the unknown all around me

the only presence that appears to stay
everything that I call mine it lent me

even the way that I believe the day
for as long as it is here and is me

Rain Light

All day the stars watch from long ago
my mother said I am going now
when you are alone you will be all right
whether or not you know you will know
look at the old house in the dawn rain
all the flowers are forms of water
the sun reminds them through a white cloud
touches the patchwork spread on the hill
the washed colors of the afterlife
that lived there long before you were born
see how they wake without a question
even though the whole world is burning

Just This

When I think of the patience I have had
back in the dark before I remember
or knew it was night until the light came
all at once at the speed it was born to
with all the time in the world to fly through
not concerned about ever arriving
and then the gathering of the first stars
unhurried in their flowering spaces
and far into the story the planets
cooling slowly and the ages of rain
then the seas starting to bear memory
the gaze of the first cell at its waking
how did this haste begin this little time
at any time this reading by lightning
scarcely a word this nothing this heaven

The Laughing Thrush

O nameless joy of the morning

tumbling upward note by note out of the night
and the hush of the dark valley
and out of whatever has not been there

song unquestioning and unbounded
yes this is the place and the one time
in the whole of before and after
with all of memory waking into it

and the lost visages that hover
around the edge of sleep
constant and clear
and the words that lately have fallen silent
to surface among the phrases of some future
if there is a future

here is where they all sing the first daylight
whether or not there is anyone listening

Animula: A Late Visitation

It must have been at some time during my years at the university that I first encountered this brief, mysterious poem. It is ascribed to the Emperor Hadrian (A.D. 76–138) without any scholarly question that I know of, but it has always seemed surprising to me that a poem so assured in its art, so flawless and so haunting, could have been the only one he ever wrote. Perhaps he wrote poems all his life and this was the only one that was saved, or this one alone was unforgettable.

Certainly, whenever I read it first, I never forgot it, and I examined each of the translations of it into English as I came across them. The one I liked best was by Dudley Fitts. But it was the original that I was happy to return to, as any reader would who could do so.

Ten years or so after I left college I read Marguerite Yourcenar's novel *Hadrian's Memoirs*, in which the poem acquires a resonant imaginary context, memorable in itself, yet it was the original poem that I went on remembering, still ignorant of the circumstances in which it had come to exist. I am not certain whose soul the poem addresses, and as far as I know no one else can be sure of that either, though of course there are rooted assumptions about it.

Although I have tried to translate poetry (in full awareness of the limitations, the utter impossibility of the enterprise) ever since those student days, it never occurred to me to attempt to import this small solitaire. But in the past years poems have come to me arising from events that recalled the familiar Latin phrases, and one day I realized that I knew, suddenly, how I would like to hear the Latin phrases in English—if they could exist in English—and the words of the translation, as they occurred to me, seemed to be as literal as they could possibly be.

About the Author

W.S. Merwin was born in New York City in 1927. From 1949 to 1951, he worked as a tutor in France, Majorca, and Portugal; for several years afterward he made the greater part of his living by translating from French, Spanish, Latin, and Portuguese. His many awards include the Pulitzer Prize in Poetry, the Lannan Lifetime Achievement Award, the Tanning Prize for mastery in the art of poetry (now the Wallace Stevens Award), the Bollingen Award, the Ruth Lilly Poetry Prize, as well as fellowships from the Rockefeller and the Guggenheim foundations and the National Endowment for the Arts. He is the author of many books of poetry and prose; his most recent volumes include *Migration: New & Selected Poems*, winner of the National Book Award, *Present Company*, winner of the Bobbitt National Prize for Poetry, *The Book of Fables*, and a new edition of *Spanish Ballads*.

He and his wife, Paula, live in Hawaii, where he has lived for more than thirty years.

Copper Canyon Press gratefully acknowledges the following individuals for generously supporting this publication:

Anonymous (2)

Sandra Aichele

Loretta Libby Atkins & Martha Jo Trolin

Denise Banker

Kristin Becker & Jeffrey Youde

Joseph Bednarik & Liesl Slabaugh

David G. Brewster & Mary Kay Sneeringer

Sarah & Tim Cavanaugh

Betsey Curran & Jonathan King

Vasiliki Dwyer

Jaune Evans

Teresa & Jim Forsyth

Mimi Gardner Gates

Mary Goldthorp

Kip & Stanley Greenthal

Art Hanlon

Kathleen Harwood

Chris Higashi

George Hitchcock & Marjorie Simon

Steven Holl & Solange Fabião

Jeanne Jenkins & Richard Baldwin

Catherine & Jim Keefe

Mary Jane Knecht

Phil Kovacevich

David Miller

Jim & Shelia Molnar

Jan North

Walter Parsons

Jessica Rice

Joseph C. Roberts

Tina Schumann

Cynthia Lovelace Sears & Frank Buxton

Rick Simonson

Two Hungry Rabbits LLC

Jim & Mary Lou Wickwire

Michael Wiegers & Kate Garfield

The Chinese character for poetry is made up of two parts: "word" and "temple." It also serves as pressmark for Copper Canyon Press.

Since 1972, Copper Canyon Press has fostered the work of emerging, established, and world-renowned poets for an expanding audience. The Press thrives with the generous patronage of readers, writers, booksellers, librarians, teachers, students, and funders—everyone who shares the belief that poetry is vital to language and living.

Major funding has been provided by:

Anonymous (2)

Sarah and Tim Cavanaugh

Beroz Ferrell & The Point, LLC

Lannan Foundation

National Endowment for the Arts

Cynthia Lovelace Sears and Frank Buxton

Washington State Arts Commission

For information and catalogs:

COPPER CANYON PRESS
Post Office Box 271
Port Townsend, Washington 98368
360-385-4925
www.coppercanyonpress.org

The Shadow of Sirius is set in Verdigris, a typeface by Mark van Bronkhorst, with titles set in Elmhurst, by Christopher Slye. Book design and composition by Valerie Brewster, Scribe Typography. Printed on archival-quality paper by Malloy Incorporated.